D1164996

This SUPER AWESOME Book Belongs to:

_____

You are becoming a scientist!

April Chloe Ferrager

Some plants are carnivorous and they trap their food. Plants that aren't carnivorous have water from the ground.

Petals

Stem

Leaf

Leaf

Roots

Brooke Shaw

Botany:
Plants, Cells, & Photosynthesis

THIS BOOK IS DEDICATED TO:

Aunt Katie Ripps

By:

April Chloe Terrazas

Botany: Plants, Cells & Photosynthesis ISBN: 978-0-9843848-7-7
April Chloe Terrazas, BS University of Texas at Austin.
Copyright © 2014 Crazy Brainz, LLC

Visit us on the web! www.Crazy-Brainz.com

Cover design, illustrations and text by: April Chloe Terrazas

This is a plant.

The 5 main parts are:
the root hairs, the roots, the leaf, the stem and terminal bud.

The terminal bud is at
the top of the plant
where new growth happens.

Root hairs are at the bottom
where they can absorb
water and nutrients from the soil.

Just like animals are made of animal cells, plants are made of plant cells.

Terminal Bud ⟶

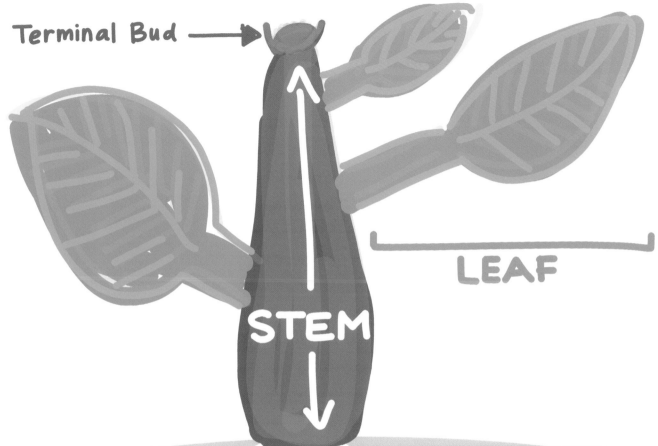

LEAF

STEM

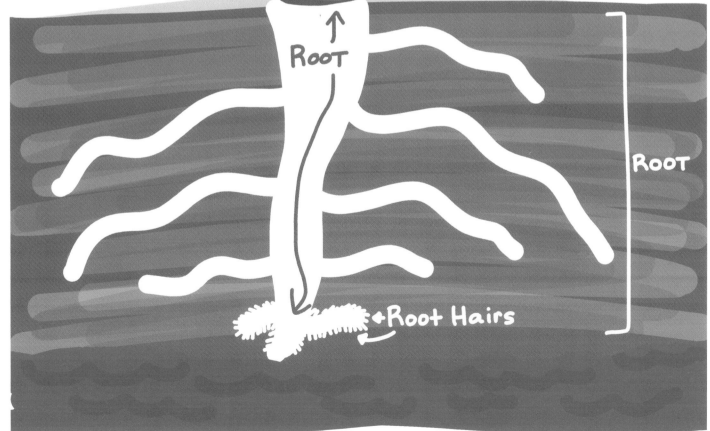

Root

ROOT

Root Hairs

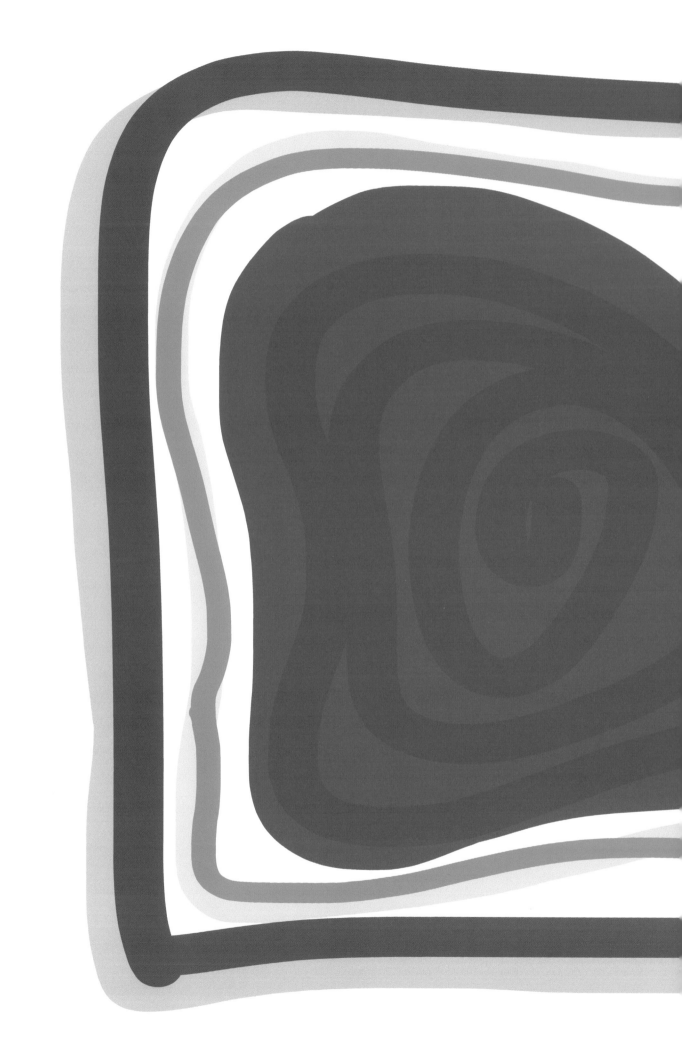

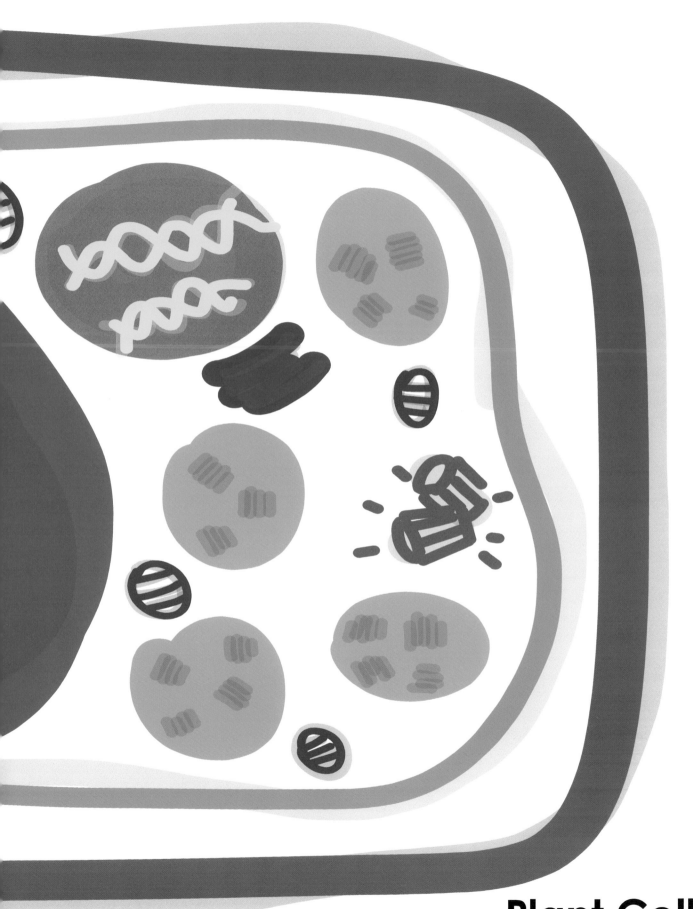

Plant Cell

This is a plant cell.

A plant cell has many of the same organelles as an animal cell.

It also has some special parts that are unique only to plant cells.

Cellulose

Sound it Out
1. SEL
2. U
3. LOS

First, look at the cell wall.
The cell wall is made of cellulose.

Plant Cell

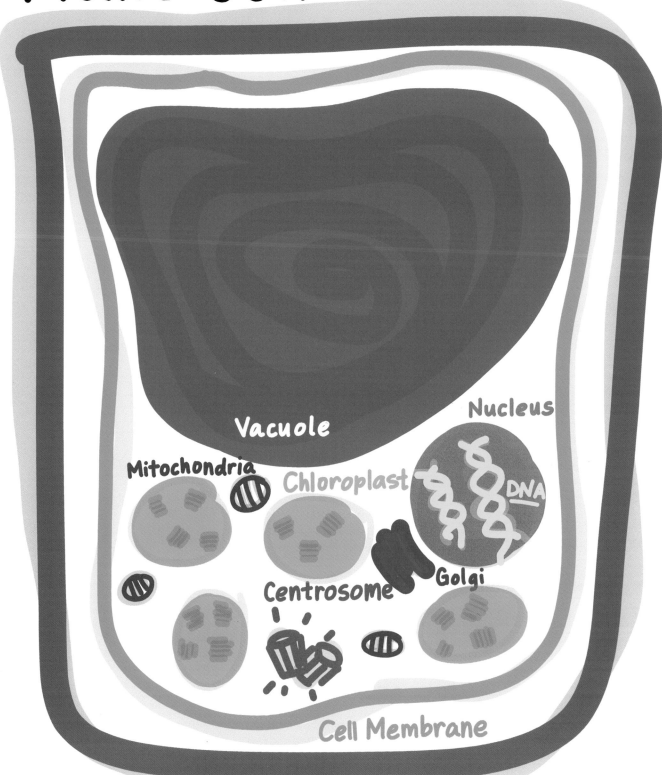

Vacuole

Nucleus

Mitochondria

Chloroplast

DNA

Centrosome

Golgi

Cell Membrane

Cell Wall (CELLULOSE)

Cellulose provides structure and shape for the cell so it can survive in nature.

Cellulose in cell walls allows plants to grow very tall!

Does a tall tree have bones like a human?

The strong cell walls act like a skeleton and make the tree big and strong.

Cellulose also helps hold up a small plant blowing in the wind.

Vacuole

Sound it Out
1. VAK
2. U
3. OL

Vacuoles are very large storage containers in plant cells.

Vacuoles store food, water and nutrients for the plant to survive.

The size of the vacuole may increase or decrease depending on how much water the plant has.

Plant Cell

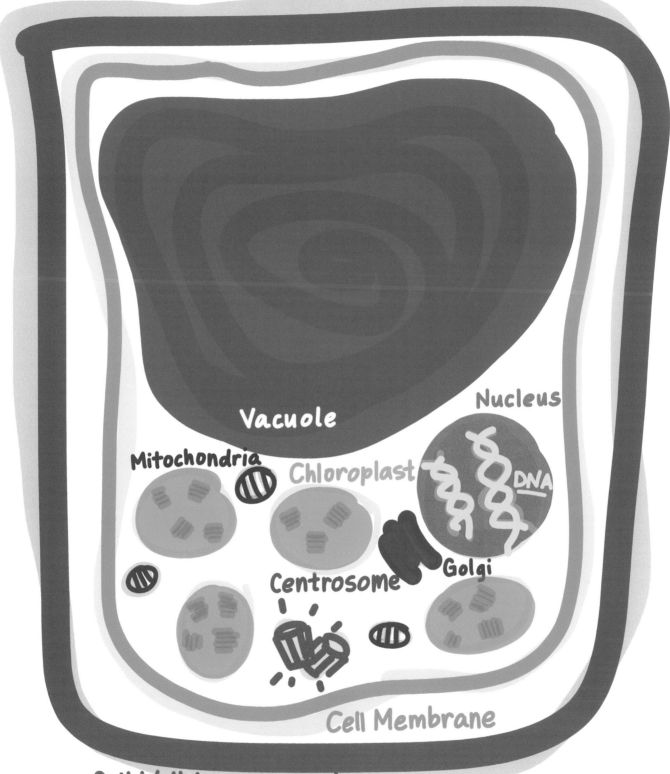

Vacuole

Nucleus

Mitochondria

Chloroplast

DNA

Centrosome

Golgi

Cell Membrane

Cell Wall (CELLULOSE)

If the plant does not have enough water, the vacuole will become small and the plant will begin to wilt. It does not have enough water and nutrients to keep it healthy.

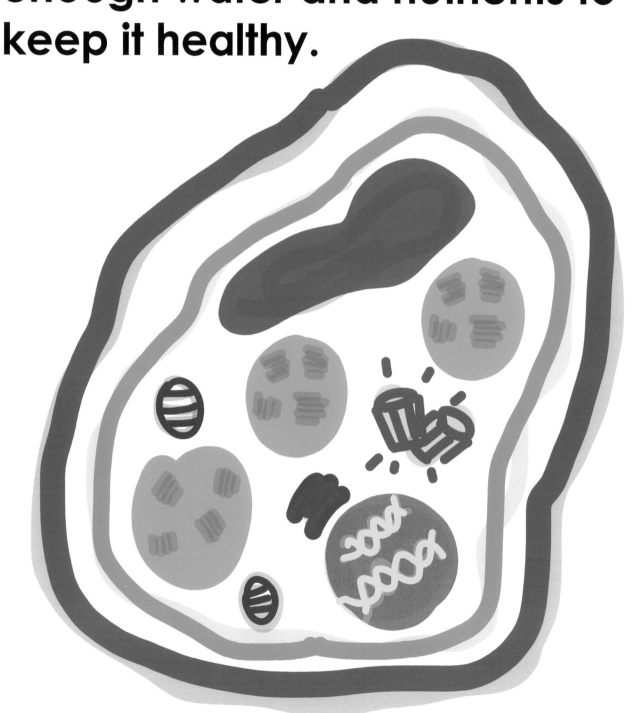

When the plant has plenty of water, the vacuole will be large, full of water and nutrients keeping the plant happy and healthy.

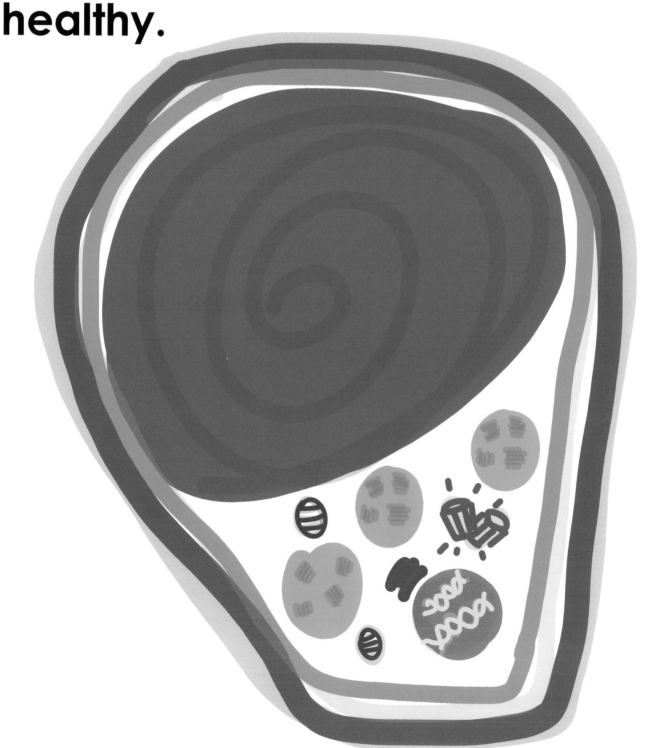

What makes plants green?

The chloroplasts!

Chloroplasts are only found in plant cells.

Chloroplast

Sound it Out
1. KLOR
2. O
3. PLAST

Chloroplasts are like chefs. Chloroplasts use ingredients to make food!

Plant Cell

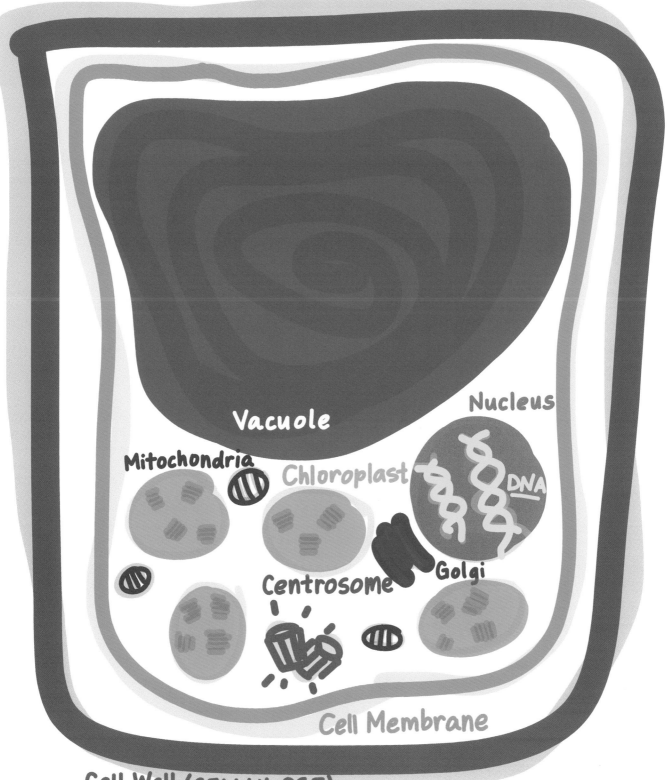

Nucleus

Vacuole

Mitochondria

Chloroplast

DNA

Centrosome

Golgi

Cell Membrane

Cell Wall (CELLULOSE)

What is cellulose? The vacuole? What are chloroplasts?

Name the parts of a plant:

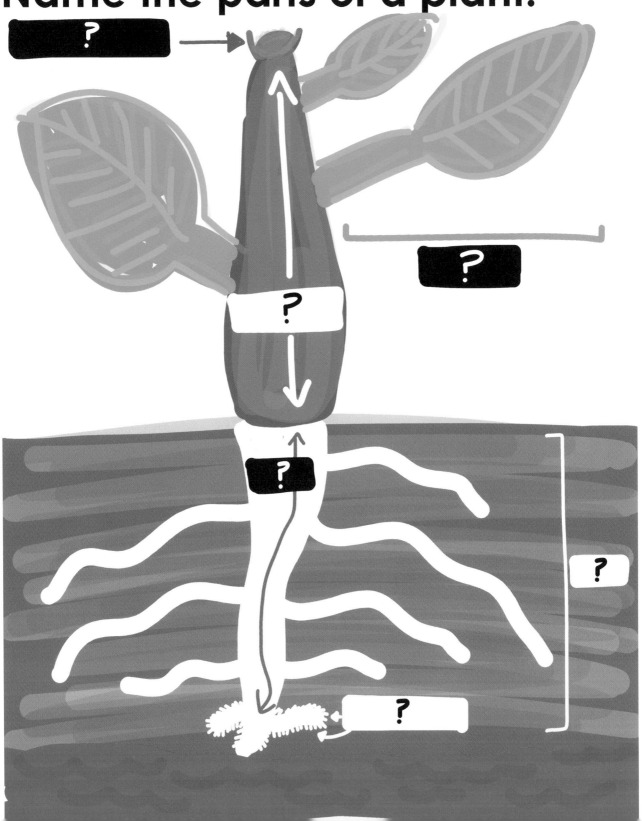

Every green plant that you see is making food using sunlight energy!

Photosynthesis is the process of chloroplasts making food using sunlight energy.

Photosynthesis

Sound it Out

1. FO
2. TO
3. SIN
4. THE
5. SIS

Photosynthesis **is really amazing!**

Chloroplasts (in the leaf of the plant) **use the following ingredients to make food:**

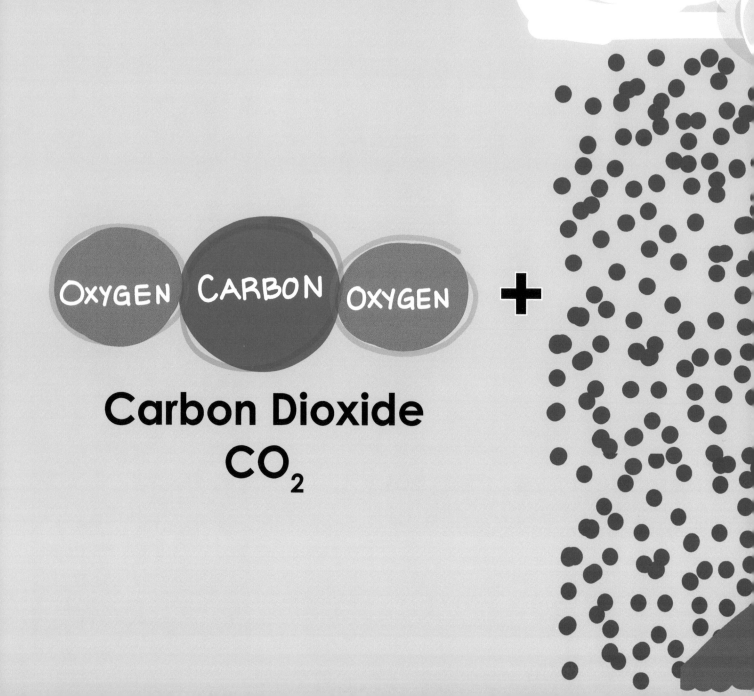

OXYGEN CARBON OXYGEN **+**

Carbon Dioxide
CO_2

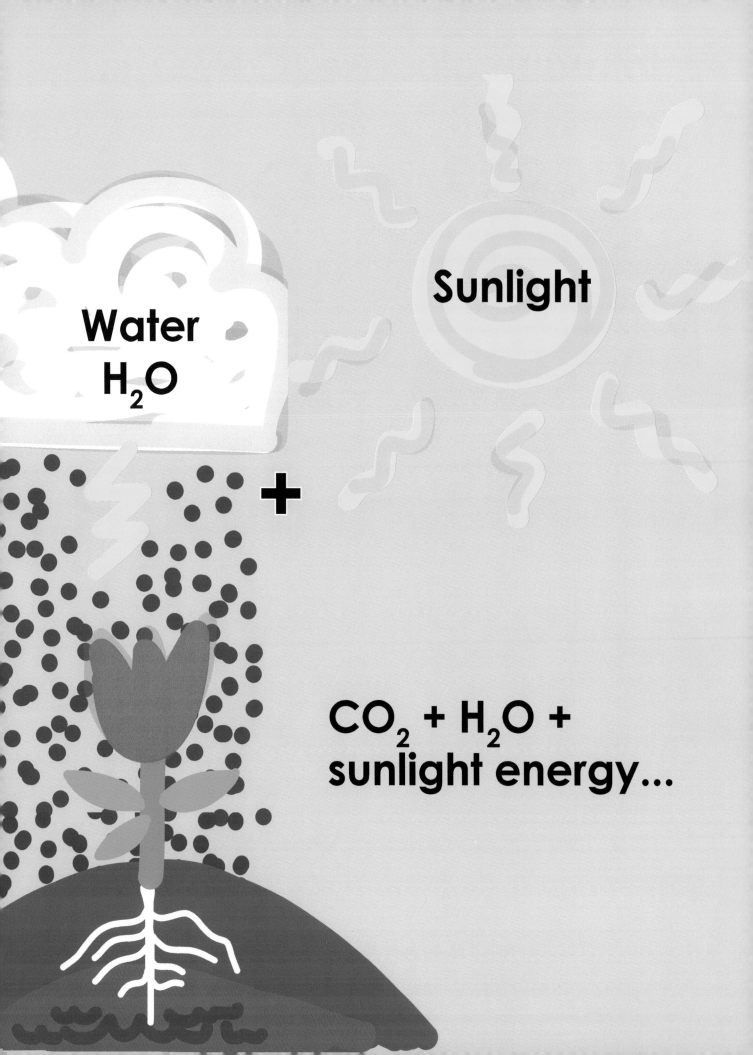

...to make glucose ($C_6H_{12}O_6$)...

Glucose

Glucose is a sugar (or food).

This is a molecule of glucose.
Glucose has 6 carbon atoms,
12 hydrogen atoms and
6 oxygen atoms.

...and oxygen gas (O_2).

The oxygen gas (O_2) that we breathe is made by plants!

+

Photosynthesis:

$CO_2 + H_2O$ + sunlight = $C_6H_{12}O_6 + O_2$

Carbon dioxide + water + sunlight = glucose + oxygen gas.

What is photosynthesis?

Where does photosynthesis happen inside the plant cell?

What are the ingredients for photosynthesis ?

What are the products of photosynthesis?

Plants get water from the ground through their roots.

How does water go from the roots to the top of a tree?

Water moves through xylem to deliver water to all of the plant cells.

Xylem is like a straw.

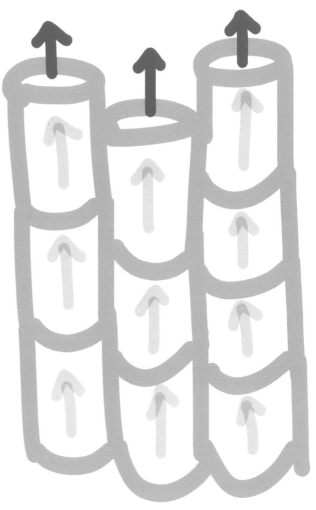

Xylem

Sound it Out

1. ZI
2. LEM

Photosynthesis in the leaves makes sugars (food).

The sugars needs to be given to all of the plant cells.

Phloem is another type of straw in the plant that moves sugars from the leaves to all of the cells in the plant, and finally to the roots.

Phloem

Sound it Out

1. FLOM

A plant has 5 main parts: root hairs, roots, stem, leaf, and terminal bud.

The plant cell is different from an animal cell because it has a cell wall made of cellulose.

Inside the plant cell, chloroplasts conduct photosynthesis to make food from ingredients!

The ingredients of photosynthesis are CO_2, H_2O and sunlight.

The products of photosynthesis are glucose and oxygen gas (O_2).

The oxygen gas (O_2) that we breathe is made by plants during photosynthesis.

Glucose is a sugar (food for the plant, and for us!)

Water moves from the ground to the roots, then through the xylem to provide water to all of the cells in the plant.

Sugars (glucose) move from the leaves (where photosynthesis takes place) to all cells in the plant and finally to the roots through the phloem.

Excellent!

Review your amazing vocabulary:

Leaf

Stem

Root

Terminal Bud

Root Hairs

Cell Wall

Cellulose

Vacuole

Chloroplast

Photosynthesis

Carbon Dioxide

Oxygen

Hydrogen

Glucose

Xylem

Phloem

You are now a Botany expert!

Draw your own plants, with xylem, phloem, **leaves, stems, roots and anything else you want to create!**

CPSIA information can be obtained
at www.ICGtesting.com
Printed in the USA
LVIC04n2134170814
399614LV00008B/21

* 9 7 8 0 9 8 4 3 8 4 8 7 7 *